FROM THE AUTHOR

Dear Reader,

When I first heard that our rainforests were being cut down, I was eight years old. It upset me so much that I convinced all my classmates to donate their lunch money to save the trees.

More than a decade later, I created a fashion brand called RainTees. I started by donating school supplies to children living in endangered rainforests and asking them to draw what they saw happening around them.

Today, RainTees features their art and, for each item sold, a tree is planted in an endangered forest. These children have amazing life stories that couldn't fit on a t-shirt. That's why I created this book, full of their beautiful drawings and words.

I invite you to journey to some of the most spectacular rainforests on our planet through the stories of three of these children, who have witnessed the destruction of these endangered ecosystems. I hope that in doing so you will be inspired, no matter where you live in the world, to help save the rainforests.

-- Beth Doane

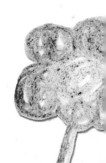

raintees ™

Visit www.raintees.com

The stories are based on real-life accounts of three children living in Central and South America. Much of the artwork in this book is original art from children living in endangered rainforests. Book design & illustration by Mel Lim Design LLC. Edited by Carole Jerome, Jenna Rose Robbins, and Katie Capri.

To all the children of Central and South America who have shown me the power of courage, love, and hope.
- B.D.

BY BETH DOANE

From the Jungle

Stories and
original art
from children
living in
rainforests

Book design
& illustration
by Mel Lim

A tree is
planted for
every book sold

Meet Mariela, Pablo, and Winnie. They each live in a beautiful, tropical jungle called a rainforest. Here the trees grow tall because it rains a lot. That's why it's called a rainforest.

Mariela

Winnie

Pablo

Layers of the Rainforest

The rainforest is divided into different layers of plant and animal life.

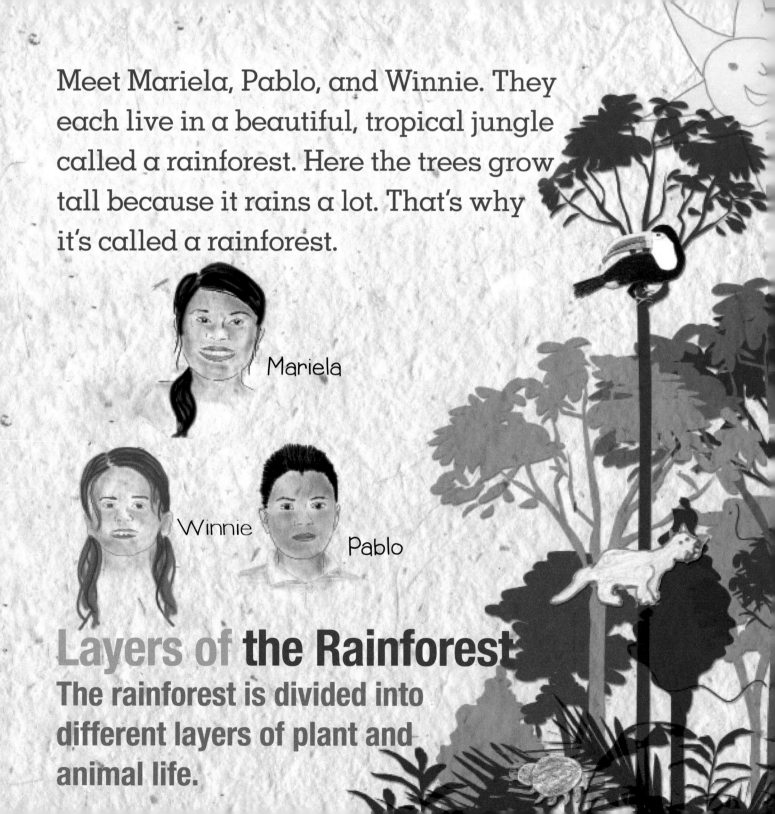

Emergent (200 feet)

Canopy (125 feet)

Understory (75 feet)

Shrub (25 feet)

Forest Floor

Rainforests are **important** because the trees help make and clean the air we breathe. These forests are also home to special trees, plants, animals, rocks, and other natural resources that can't be found anywhere else on the planet.

Some call the rainforests the **"jewels of the Earth."**

That means they are treasures.

United States
Mexico
ATLANTIC OCEAN
PACIFIC OCEAN
Venezuela
Guyana
Colombia
Suriname
French Guia
Costa Rica
Ecuador
Peru
Brazil
Bolivia
Chile
Paragua
Argentina
Uruguay

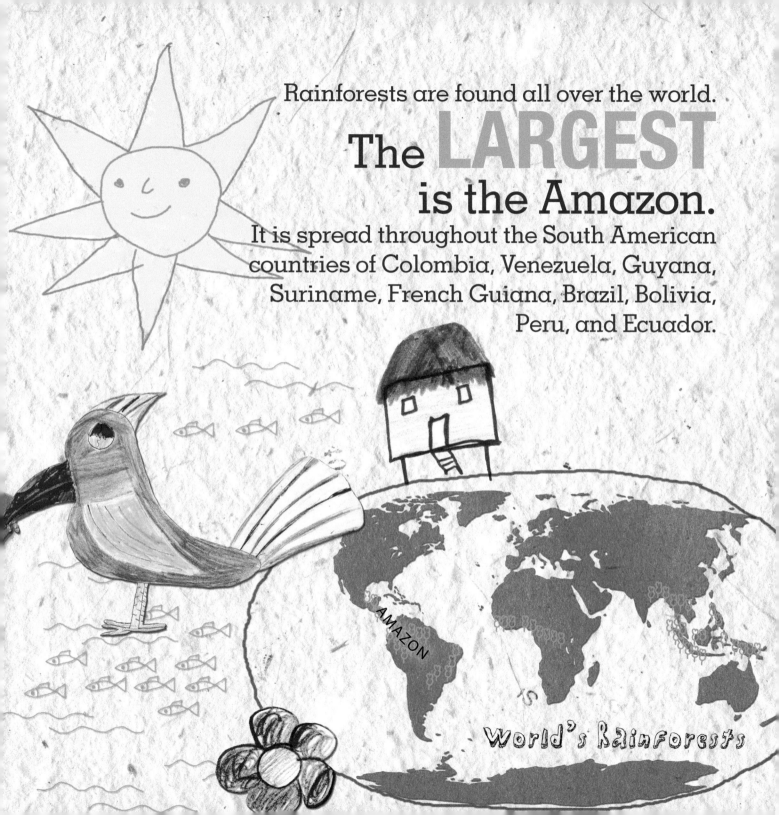

Rainforests are found all over the world. The **LARGEST** is the Amazon. It is spread throughout the South American countries of Colombia, Venezuela, Guyana, Suriname, French Guiana, Brazil, Bolivia, Peru, and Ecuador.

AMAZON

World's Rainforests

Who else lives in the rainforest?

Animals teach us about life on our planet, and rainforests are home to thousands of animals – frogs and lizards, giant monkeys and panthers, and many others. The forests are also home to lots of special plants that can help people who are sick.

Some people look at the rainforests and miss seeing the beauty. All they see are things they can sell to make money.

They cut down the trees to make furniture, clothing, and paper.

When people cut down the rainforests, the animals and plants have no place to live. They go away and we don't get to see or learn about them. They may even die if they don't have a habitat.

There are thousands of plants and animals still waiting to be discovered in the rainforests.

We don't want them to vanish before we even meet them.

Let's follow Mariela, Winnie, and Pablo into their beautiful jungles.

They want to show us what they see people doing to their rainforests in Central and South America.

United States

Mexico

Winnie - 10 years old.
I live in Manuel Antonio
in Costa Rica.

Costa Rica

Pablo - 12 years old.
I live in the Amazon
in Tena, Ecuador.

Ecuador

Mariela - 15 years old.
I live in the forest of
El Chino in Peru.

Peru

My name is Mariela and I am 15 years old.

I live in the country of Peru, in a small jungle village called El Chino deep within the Amazon rainforest.

My house has a thatched roof made of palm tree branches, which we dry out in the sun for many days. They keep our house very cool and dry. These branches come from trees in the rainforest.

When I was younger, an oil
company came into our village!
They cut down trees,
including our palm trees,
to drill for oil!

When they brought oil up out
of the ground, it leaked into
the land and rivers, and
poisoned people and animals.

My father is a fisherman who catches fish from small boats in the rivers by my home.

There used to be thousands of fish in these rivers, until giant fishing boats arrived. They put their big nets into the water and pulled out hundreds of fish all at once. The big boats left hardly any fish for my dad.

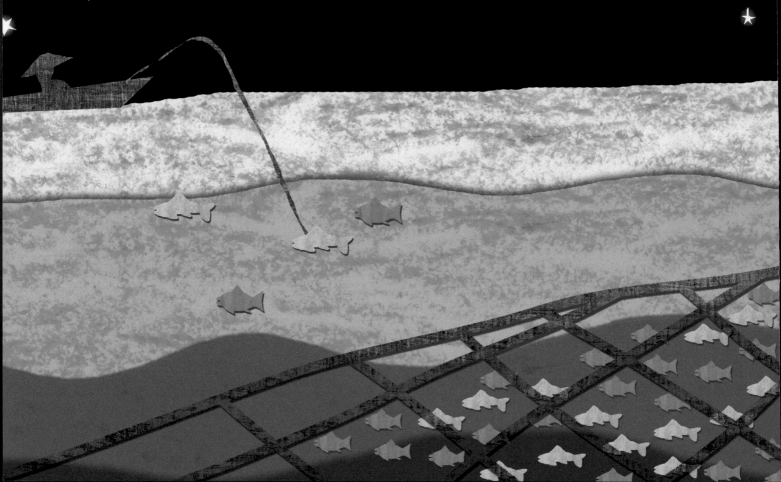

But one day, we learned our village
had been made into a nature reserve.
Now the rivers have cleared up,
the fish have returned, and we
are all much happier.

A nature reserve is a protected area of **wildlife and ecosystems.**

An ecosystem is a community of all sorts of creatures - plants, birds, animals, people, water, soil, fish, trees, and natural resources – who share the same environment and live in harmony.

My name is Pablo and I am 12 years old. I live in a little village called Tena, in the country of Ecuador.

Every day I ride to school by riverboat with the other children in my village.

We don't have cars or paved roads in our village, so we use the water like a road.

It's hot in the jungle all year long, so my friends and I play in the river to cool off.

Sometimes people come to our village to capture baby monkeys and other wild animals. Then they sell the animals to circuses, zoos, or pet stores.

This makes me sad. No animal should be taken from its home or family.

I hope that some day
people will see that it's best
to keep animals in their
jungle home.

My name is Winnie and I am 10 years old. I live in the rainforest of Manuel Antonio in Costa Rica. The weather is a warm 70-80 degrees all year long.

I always have wild
monkeys, iguanas, butterflies,
toucans, and small spotted leopards
called "ocelots" around my house.

My favorite monkeys are the mono titi. They are small and friendly brown monkeys with little white faces.

The mono titi are endangered. That means that only a few thousand are left in the entire world. And all of them live right here in Manuel Antonio!

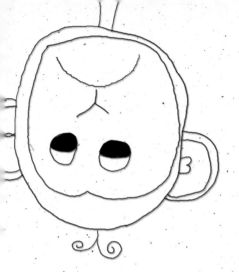

It makes me sad to see people cutting down rainforests to build big hotels and new homes.

Where will the animals
live if we take away
their forest?

Without trees to live in, the little mono titi will become extinct — just like the dinosaurs.

The world of people is **dangerous** for the mono titi.

The little monkeys don't know how to cross roads safely or that they shouldn't swing on electrical lines.

Along with other children who live nearby, I help the mono titi by building "monkey bridges."

OUCH!

Monkey bridges are bright blue. The mono titi learn that these bridges are safe and only for them.

So far we have built more than 130 bridges, which scientists say are saving the mono titi. And just think, a local child came up with the idea!

What ideas do you have for helping the rainforests?

HOW CAN I HELP SAVE THE RAINFORESTS?

FOR KIDS

1. Have a Rainforest Fundraiser

Gather a group of kids from your classroom or neighborhood and hold a bake sale, a car wash, or a rummage sale. Then, donate the money to save the rainforest.

To see a list of organizations you can write or donate to, visit www.raintees.com/FromTheJungle

2. Write a Letter

Writing letters is a very powerful way to let people know how you feel about a subject. By taking the time to personally write letters to companies that destroy the rainforest, you may be able to help them realize how important it is not to cut them down.

3. Use Paper Wisely

An easy way to save the rainforest is to use less paper, because most paper comes from trees. When you do use paper, always recycle it or use it for something else, like an art project or for cleaning up. If you don't have a recycle box in your house or school, create one! You can save hundreds of trees every year by recycling paper.

HOW CAN I HELP TO SAVE THE RAINFORESTS?

FOR ADULTS

1. Try to buy wood and paper products that are certified by the FSC (Forest Stewardship Council, www.fsc.org). The FSC makes sure that these products do not come from tropical rainforests.

2. Start using products that are gasoline and plastic free. Oil is a main component of these products, and industrial oil is often extracted from rainforests.

3. Cycle, walk, or ride public transportation whenever possible.

4. Always remember to recycle household items such as bottles, cans, newspapers, magazines, and food packages. Before making a purchase, check to see if the packaging is recyclable.

5. Eat more vegetables. Many cattle and other meat animals graze in large commercial pastures created by burning hundreds of acres of rainforests. Find out where your meat comes from. Ask your local grocery store to buy sustainable and locally raised meat products.

What do you see around you?

Draw, write, or take a picture about saving the environment and the Earth. Hang it on your wall or in your classroom to share with others, or send your artwork to us so that we can share it too!

Mail your art to:

RainTees
1507 7th Street #58
Santa Monica, CA
90401

Balboa Press books may be ordered through booksellers or by contacting:

Balboa Press
A Division of Hay House
1663 Liberty Drive
Bloomington, IN 47403
www.balboapress.com
1-(877) 407-4847

ISBN: 978-1-4525-6091-5 (e)
ISBN: 978-1-4525-6090-8 (sc)

Library of Congress Control Number: 2012921308

Printed in the United States of America

Balboa Press rev. date: 11/21/2012

BALBOA
PRESS
A DIVISION OF HAY HOUSE

Printed in the United States
by Baker & Taylor Publisher Services